The High School Survival Guide

Start Your Journey on the Right Path

Kristi Reirden Donay

authorHOUSE

1663 LIBERTY DRIVE, SUITE 200
BLOOMINGTON, INDIANA 47403
(800) 839-8640
WWW.AUTHORHOUSE.COM

AuthorHouse™
1663 Liberty Drive, Suite 200
Bloomington, IN 47403
www.authorhouse.com
Phone: 1-800-839-8640

AuthorHouse™ UK Ltd.
500 Avebury Boulevard
Central Milton Keynes, MK9 2BE
www.authorhouse.co.uk
Phone: 08001974150

©2006 Kristi Reirden Donay. All rights reserved.

No part of this book may be reproduced, stored in a retrieval system, or transmitted by any means without the written permission of the author.

First published by AuthorHouse 3/9/2006

ISBN: 1-4208-8993-1 (sc)

Library of Congress Control Number: 2005908994

Printed in the United States of America
Bloomington, Indiana

This book is printed on acid-free paper.

Acknowledgments:

Thank you to my family for their support throughout this endeavor.

Take Responsibility for Your Learning

Anyone can have the skills of a good student. They do not require hours of learning, but they do require a bit of dedication, some planning, and a desire to make learning a priority. Good academic students know how to do the following things:

- Take responsibility for their role in the learning process.
- Are ACTIVE members of the learning process.
- Get themselves organized.
- Learn about themselves to become more effective students.
- Are good self advocates.
- Set goals and create a plan of action to meet them.
- Understand that teachers don't give grades, students earn them.

Why should this be important to you?

- The more effective you are at studying the less time you waste in the process.
- Being prepared should make the education process feel less overwhelming.
- The more positive your educational experience, the less stress you have as a student. In many cases a student's educational stress also has a direct link to stress levels at home.
- You are in High School now, and from the beginning all of your GRADES COUNT!

Learn the skills necessary to become a successful student, and you will use them the rest of your life!

Less time wasted = more time for you!
**(This is your bonus for getting organized
and setting your priorities in line.)**

Invest in Yourself

Table of Contents

I. Organize yourself for the learning process 1

II. Understanding how you learn 9

III. Day-to-day strategies 15

IV. Preparing for tests 31

V. Other pearls 49

I.

Organize yourself for the learning process

Organization

Why should organization be important to you?

➢ It will save you time and energy looking for lost materials.

➢ Allows you to get started each day and each evening without feeling lost about <u>what</u> to do.

➢ Allows you to be on top of your life and to demonstrate that fact to your teachers and your parents.

➢ Once again, less time wasted = <u>more flexibility with your time!</u>

The Basics of School Organization

I. Organize yourself for the daily life of being a student:

1. Get an assignment notebook.

2. Copy your class schedule and put it in the front of your assignment notebook. Identify where you have built in study time during the day and <u>use it!</u>

3. Determine what your schedule is for the day and only carry the materials necessary. (For example, if you have math in the afternoon, why carry your math books and assignments with you all morning?)

4. Identify what the teacher's expectations are for your materials in each particular class. If they want you to have a spiral bound notebook, get that, not a folder with loose-leaf paper in it. Teachers have reasons for requiring specific materials.

5. Once you have obtained their list of materials use the following suggestions to increase your organization:

   - Color-code the notebooks, folders, spiral notebooks etc... for each class.
   - Mark each notebook, folder, spiral notebook with your name, the class, and the teacher's name.

- Keep a pocket folder to place all completed assignments in, so that they will not get misplaced prior to handing them in.
- Keep a folder for miscellaneous papers that you are not sure where to put. This will help to keep your bag, or backpack, under control.

6. Keep a plastic pouch, or some sort of bag, in your backpack with all your pens, pencils, highlighters, etc…
7. Make sure that you <u>date</u> and <u>label</u> your notes. Identify the class activity: lecture, slide presentation, guest speaker, video…

II. The Assignment Notebook

The all important assignment notebook, date book, or calendar – whatever term you prefer to use. This is the <u>essential tool in getting yourself organized</u> and staying on top of assignments. *So now you have it – make sure you use it.* Here are some tips and strategies to get the most out of your assignment book.

1. Write down all assignments immediately as they are announced. If your teacher writes them on the board everyday at the beginning of class <u>so should you</u>.
2. Write your classes down in your book the same order each day. You can chose whatever order works for you but <u>be consistent</u>.
   - Many students like to write them in the order they occur during the day
   - Some chose to put them in order of difficulty.
3. For larger assignments write down the day they are due, and then break the assignments up into smaller chunks. Give yourself due dates for each section – this will help you avoid procrastinating until the last second.
4. Do not just write down academic related information. Write down anything that occurs in your life; clubs, extracurricular activities, part-time jobs, etc…..

5. Review the day's assignments as you are packing your bag to take home for the night.
6. When sitting down to complete your homework it can be helpful to predict the amount of time each assignment should take you and then prioritize them. This will help you to manage your time more wisely.
7. Cross out completed assignments, and immediately place them in the works completed folder.

* Electronic planners can also be great tools as long as you use them consistently. The suggestions above should still be applied.

Example of how a student may write down their daily assignments:

Monday 14th

Biology – Read and answer questionnaire. Due tomorrow.

Trigonometry – Complete all the problems in page 104-106. Due tomorrow

English – Paper on the Crucible assigned due in 2 weeks. Finish reading the Crucible for class Wed.

History – Read and annotate chapter 6. Write down 3 ideas for presentation on the Civil Rights Movement.

French – Learn all vocab in Ch.4. Exam on Friday-

Other:
   Practice after school. Tutor for French at 6:00

Sample for how to review and begin the planning process prior to starting your work.

Monday 14th

4. Biology – <u>Read</u> and <u>answer questionnaire</u>. Due tomorrow. *30 min.*

1. Trigonometry – Complete all the problems in page 104-106. Due tomorrow. *30 min.*

5. English – Paper on the <u>Crucible</u> due in 2 weeks. Finish reading the <u>Crucible</u> for class Wed. *30 min.*
    Map out plan timeline*

2. History – <u>Read</u> and <u>annotate</u> Ch. 6. Write down <u>3 ideas for presentation</u> on the Civil Rights Movement. *45 min.*

3. French – Learn all vocab in Ch. 4 <u>Exam on Friday</u>-
    * plan study time for the rest of the week

Other:
    Practice after school. Tutor for French at 6:00 *15 min.*

When planning your study time for the evening or after school it may help to underline key words or phrases in the assignments. Number them in order of difficulty or in terms of what you will accomplish first, second, so on...

- Make notes for yourself about long term assignments.
- Use a different color to identify important things.
- Always check off each assignment as completed.

Lastly, before you begin your study activities for the night, <u>write out your plan of action</u>. Include in your plan all of your evening activities, from dinner to talking with your friends. Allot yourself enough time for projects, assignments, and study breaks. Follow your plan, and cross of items as they are completed.

A note about extracurricular activities:

Many students choose to participate in extracurricular activities either through the school or outside of the school setting. These are very important activities which teach us many valuable lessons. They help us to foster skills other than those taught in the classroom. They require students to be conscientious about their time management and the commitments they make. <u>Know what the expectations are of your academic life</u>, and then find out the expectations required of the outside activities (sports, theater, music, jobs….) <u>before making too many commitments</u>. As you continue through the education process you will need to practice managing all your activities in combination with managing the academic rigors of high school and beyond. Put academics first, because your success there will open doors throughout your life. In most educational institutions the school activities require you to meet predetermined academic standards. Do not put yourself in a situation where your academics prevent you from participating, thus letting your peers down.

Thinking of Sports beyond High School?

Facts you need to keep in mind:

Governing Associations:

NCAA – National Collegiate Athletic Association
NJCAA – National Junior College Athletic Association
NAIA – National Association of Intercollegiate Athletics

Scholarships can be offered by NCAA schools which maintain a division I or II status, however not directly for sports in Division III. NAIA schools may award athletic scholarships, as can Division I and II NJCAA schools. Guidelines can be viewed via the internet at the following sites: www.ncaa.org , www.naia.org , and www.njcaa.org

No NCAA or NAIA school, regardless of how talented you are, can accept you if you cannot pass the "clearing house" which looks to make sure your transcripts and test scores meet the predetermined regulations for playing sports in college. The standards set forth by the governing bodies are continually updated and reflect a strong emphasis on solid, well rounded education. For example, the core number of classes required by the NCAA will increase in 2005 and 2008. Each requires a core number of classes be taken with a minimum GPA for those classes. They also each have predetermined ACT/SAT scores. For a more detailed account of what core classes must be taken to ensure eligibility see the above websites.

II.

Understanding how you learn

It's all about Style
Learning Styles

Why should you know what kind of learner you are?

Knowing what kind of learner you are will help you decide how to study. Knowing the best way to study for YOU will increase your efficiency. In other words, you will waste less time getting the material to stay where you want it – in your brain. It will also allow you to take your classroom notes, textbooks, etc. and redesign them to your particular style.

Attacking problems with the right approach will help you study more effectively and efficiently. It will help you in selecting classes and, when possible, teachers. For example, if you learn best by seeing information put on the overhead or board, you will want to avoid classes that have teachers that only lecture. This is particularly important as you leave the high school academic field, where your choices may be limited, and move into a college or post high school setting.

On the next page you will see a list of items that will help you to determine the type of learner you are. There are many other types of learning styles, but these three general styles will help you determine more about your learning. Circle the statements that you feel describe you best. The more items you have circled in a particular category indicates which styles you naturally gravitate towards.

Visual (likes to learn by reading and observing)	Auditory (Likes to learn by listening)	Kinesthetic/Hands On (likes to learn by doing)
Remembers things best in graphs, pictures, diagrams	Reads best when reading out loud	Likes to learn by doing things with the material.
Would prefer to sit back and observe rather than participate	Likes to say the problems out loud when working math problems	Remembers best when actively doing something like drawing or note taking
Would rather read independently than have information read to you	Easily remembers songs, stories, jokes, and other extraneous information	Enjoys making things, putting things together
Does best when directions are written instead of spoken	Sounding out words usually comes easy	You remember how to spell words if you trace them with your finger, or use your fingers when doing math.
Finds it easier to take notes from the board than from a lecture	Follow directions the best when they are said out loud	Likes taking things apart and putting them together.
Uses visualization to remember information	Prefers classes that allow for lots of discussion	Would prefer a project verses a paper assignment
When someone asks you to spell a word, you need to write it down.	Remember things the best when you create a song or rhyme to learn the information	Often gets easily bored when reading
Tend to wander off sometimes during lectures.	Likes to talk to others and to self out loud	You prefer to move around when you talk.
Likes to read	Sometimes distracted by noise	I remember a phone number better if you press the numbers when trying to recall it.
Notices details		

While you need to be flexible within the classroom setting, one advantage to understanding more about what works for you is the ability to study in your best modality. Take what the teacher and the texts give you and make it work for you.

Below are some sample activities that fit best with the three learning styles.

Visual (likes to learn by reading and observing)	Auditory (Likes to learn by listening)	Kinesthetic/Hands On (likes to learn by doing)
Color code you notes, flashcards etc.	Tape record your class	Type your notes
Read all the pictures and charts associated with readings	Tape record yourself reading and replay	Draw charts, pictures or graphs as you read or listen in class to make the activity active
Make charts, pictures, graphic organizers…	Study with a partner or in groups	When memorizing information it may be helpful to walk around as you look at your notes, flashcards etc.
Practice visualization techniques	Have your parents or friends quiz you	Take notes in class
Highlight, underline, circle important information	Read out loud	Break down large concepts and put them into pieces that fit together.
Number steps and lists in a different color to make is visually significant	Use verbal repetition to remember	Make puzzles to remember information
	Always read directions out loud to yourself	
	Ask a lot of questions	

III.

Day-to-day strategies

Day-to-day Success Strategies

- To be successful in school you must <u>go to class</u>! (sorry to state the obvious)
- Be <u>on time</u> to class.
- Demonstrate a <u>respectful attitude</u> towards <u>all</u> your teachers.
- Do your work.
- Be an <u>active participant</u> in class.
- Make sure you have the recommended materials and are organized for your classes.
- Become an <u>effective listener</u>.
- Immediately <u>communicate</u> with your teachers if you are concerned about an assignment, content in the class, test preparation, or any returned assignments or assessments.

Strategies for becoming an effective listener

- <u>Sit close to the front of the classroom whenever possible</u>. This is important for students who are easily distracted as well as any other student wanting to make it easier to concentrate on what the teacher is saying.
- It is important to be able to not only <u>hear</u> your teacher but to <u>see</u> your teacher. This will again help you to focus on his/her words.
- Concentrate on what is said in classroom discussions and lectures.
- If you get distracted remind yourself where you are and that you should be listening.

- As you are listening, think, what do you already know about the subject and evaluate <u>how what is being said can be connected to what you already know.</u>
- Take thorough notes.
- **Become and active listener – it will increase your focus!**

    *this means do something as your teacher lectures – take notes; make graphs and charts, etc.

- **Listen and look for the signals** your teacher sends indicating important information. Some examples may be:
    - "This is important...."
    - "Write this down..."
    - The teacher writes information on the board as he/she speaks.
    - The teacher may show a change in voice tone or energy during the most critical pieces of information. Pay attention to these changes.
    - Slowing down and repeating key words and phrases are also good indicators of important information.

<u>**Active listening**</u> usually entails note taking. There are many strategies for taking notes. It is important to find out what works for you. This may be class dependent or style dependent.

Some basic note taking tips:
- Write down the teachers main points in your own words. Use important vocabulary, combined with language you would use, when describing the same point.
- Do not try to write down everything that is said in class.
- Focus on the listening cues to determine what is important.

WAKE UP AND WRITE!

Teachers' words are great clues!

Today we are going to	There are two parts…
This is important because...	Follow these steps…
In Summary...	Three characteristics specific to…
In conclusion…	Two ways to identify the …
The key point is….	There are several categories of…
The difference is…	If you compared….

- Try to answer the Who, What, Where, Why, When and How questions. Then add to that <u>So What</u>? In other words, why is this important to me or why should this be important to me?

- If the teacher writes something on the board – you should too!

- Leave the left hand margin open for questions you want to ask later or during an appropriate break in the lecture.

So what's next?

Always review your notes. It may be helpful to rewrite them and put them in a format more conducive to your learning style for studying later on. The simple act of reorganizing the information is a great study technique. Some ways to organize information include:

Annotate your notes:

- Color code, underline, circle, or highlight the main points and definitions of the days lecture.
- Number details associated with each point.
- Add your own personal knowledge in the margins; this will help you to link information to your memory more effectively.
- Replace any abbreviations or shorthand with full words.

Recreate the information:

- Create a concept map or graphic organizer.
- Write information in an outline format.
- Draw a timeline.
- Draw pictures that coincide with material.
- Create your own form.

Concept Maps and Graphic Organizers:

Concepts maps are great tools for rewriting your notes or to help you study for a test. This is especially effective for those of you that are more visual and kinesthetic in nature. Here are some sample constructs with hints as to their best use.

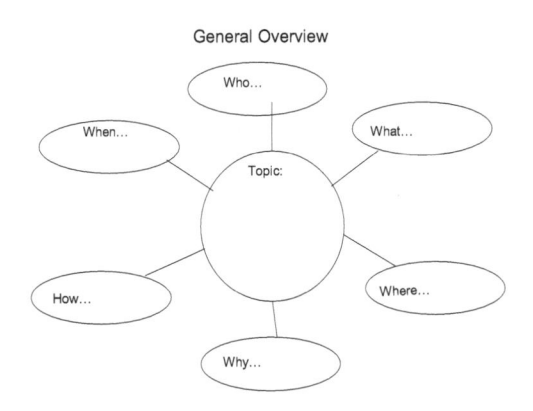

General Overview

- Who...
- When...
- What...
- Topic:
- How...
- Where...
- Why...

Good for general information from a book, text, or lecture.

Create Charts

Similarities		
Differences		

Helps in preparing compare and contrast essays.

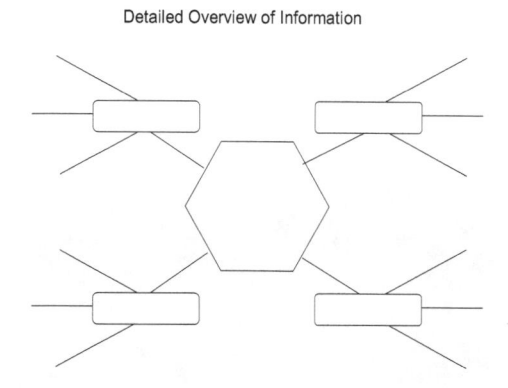

Detailed Overview of Information

Good for a main topic with multiple subtopics, plus details and descriptions.

Characteristics/Details Chart

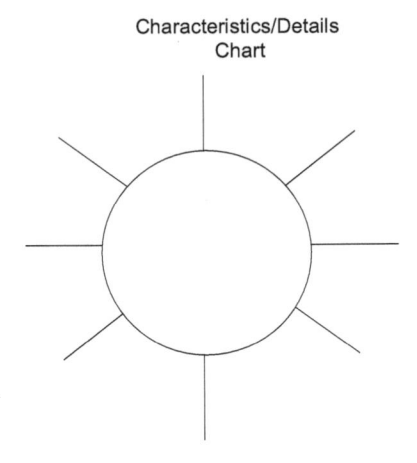

Good for collecting details about a single topic.

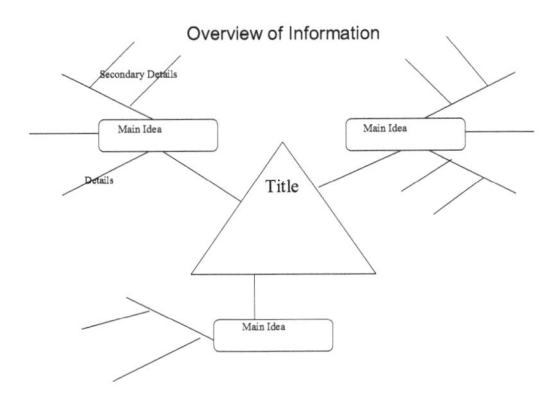

Overview of Information

Good for establishing relationships in novels and stories.

The High School Survival Guide   23

Cyclical Information

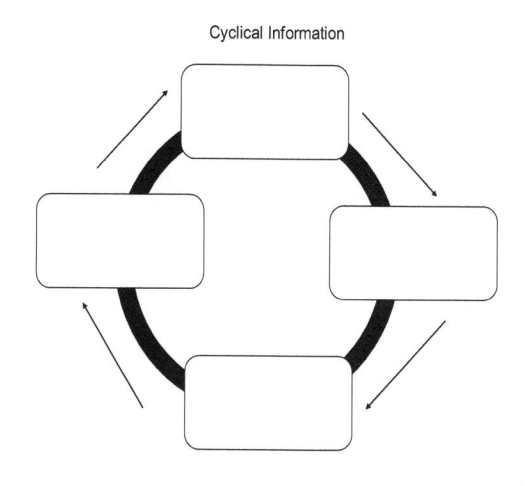

Helps to visually display circular patterns.

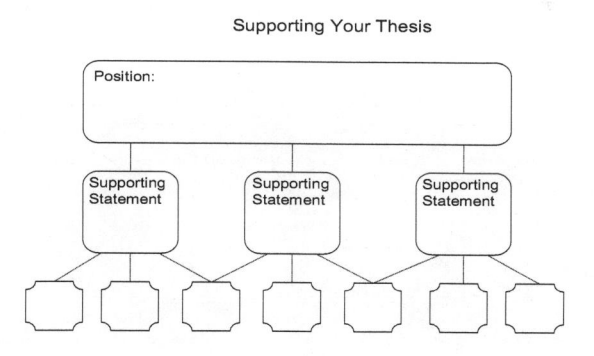

Supporting Your Thesis

Position:

Supporting Statement | Supporting Statement | Supporting Statement

A great tool for organizing your ideas when writing a paper.

Cause and Effect Data

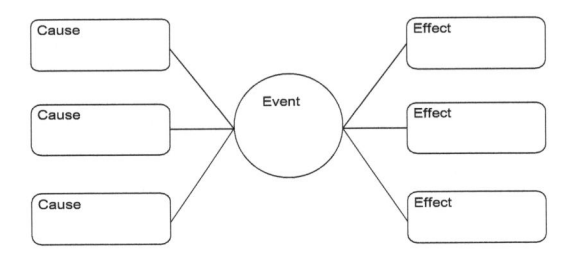

```
[Cause]                    [Effect]
         \                /
[Cause] —— (Event) ——   [Effect]
         /                \
[Cause]                    [Effect]
```

Good for establishing pre-post information, connections, or relationships.

Order of Importance

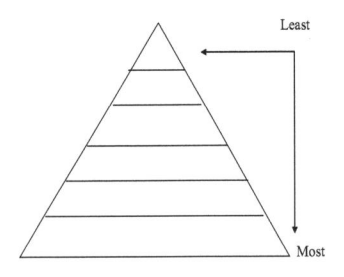

A pyramid divided into horizontal sections, with "Least" labeled at the top and "Most" at the bottom, and an arrow pointing down along the right side.

Ideal for visually depicting hierarchical information.

Outline formats:

Formal

I. Main topic

    A. Subtopic
        1. Detail
        2. Detail
    B. Subtopic
        1. Detail
        2. Detail

Informal

1. Topic
_____
_____
_____

2. 2nd Topic
_____
_____

List details below topic

Timelines and Sequencing

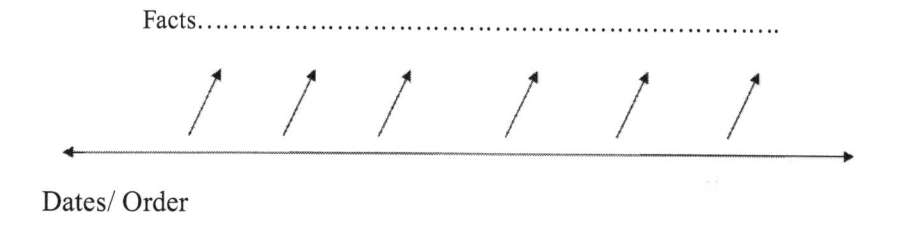

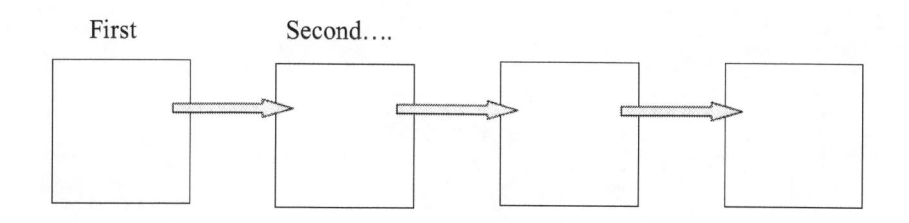

Facts...

Dates/ Order

First   Second....

Freeform

Draw what makes the material memorable for you. Design a picture that links the information in a meaningful way.

How to read your textbooks/ class reading assignments

The most effective way to retain the information you read is by becoming an <u>active reader</u>. To become an <u>active reader</u> you must <u>participate</u> in the reading process.

How do you do that?

First, ask yourself these three basic questions before you begin to read:

1. Why am I reading this?

2. What information do I already know about this topic?

3. Is there a specific assignment linked to this reading? (If you need to answer questions related to the reading, always review them prior to reading.)

Ways to become an active reader include:

1. Annotating

If your teacher assigns a specific form of annotating you should use what they expect. Otherwise annotating can be simply defined as making notes in the margin of what you read. Annotating is great to use in combination with the other tools discussed in this book. So what should you write or make note of?

- Important details
- Personal responses - your opinions and thoughts
- Questions that arise
- Associations with other information pertinent to the class
- Significance of facts
- Create a summary

- Character descriptions
- Note reoccurring themes
- Symbols
- Identify plot
- Unfamiliar vocabulary
- Who, What, Where, Why, When, How ... So What?
- Predictions
- Note new information presented in the section.
- Important dialogue you may need for writing papers or supporting a thesis...

* While annotating may seem to slow down the reading process it will save you time as you study and is an effective tool in learning the material you read.

2. Underline/Highlighting

Use this to call attention to important details and information in the section. It may also be helpful to number details as you read. Put a star by the main theme. Circle important people identified in the text. Create a pattern that works for you, but always use the same system. Some key points:

- Read through the section before you begin to highlight.
- Use highlighting to make <u>major points</u> stand out.
- Highlight terms written in bold.
- Highlight new terminology and definitions.
- Do not get carried away, about 15-20% of the information is typically sufficient.
- Highlighted information can help you create lists, note cards, maps, outlines, etc...

3. Diagramming or creating charts/graphic organizers

This is particularly helpful for visual learners. Use it to recreate what you read. Earlier in this section examples of graphic organizers were given but be creative, think of what links this information to you in a visual sense. For example, if there is scientific information dealing with levers and pulley systems create pictures that follow the format discussed in your text or in class. <u>Create a visual image that means something to you and it will be easier to remember.</u>

4. Create a color coding system

Use specific colors to designate lists of information, words, people, etc. When reading use colors to identify details.

5. A Basic Reading Effectiveness Strategy

Skim to familiarize yourself with the section you are reading. Reread looking for important new information. Write a summary for yourself.

Many of these skills are all discussed in the "note taking and review your notes section" because they are skills that apply to all academics. They are skills that should be used across the board, in preparation, note taking, reading, and studying. If you use these skills effectively you will be more likely to learn, retain, and recall the information. The best thing you can do for yourself is find something that works for you. It doesn't have to fit a single model. Blend them together, or create your own. The key is to **GET ACTIVE**!

IV. Preparing for tests

A Basic overview

Test Taking Tips

- Make sure you **read all the directions**. <u>Underline</u> or circle the **key components**.
- Answer the questions you're sure of first.
- On the back of your test write down any information you are concerned you might forget as you move forward in the test, such as formulas or acronyms.
- **Recheck** each answer for careless mistakes.
- Don't study globally – **study with a point** – the main point.
- **Identify the main topics** and **use "wh" questions** when studying.
- **Color-code** your notes.
- <u>Underline</u> key words in test questions, such as <u>**"wh" statements**</u>, or <u>**directives**</u>. (Example: compare and contrast, discuss, identify…)
- Know what your teacher *emphasized* – they do that to clue you into important information.
- In order for a statement to be true – **all of the statement must be true**.
(Watch for words such as all, never, always etc…)
- When answering matching questions answer the ones you are sure of first, **crossing off the answers you used**.
- When writing an essay, construct answers around **who, what, where, when, how, why, and "so what?"**.
- **In this case looks usually do matter!** If you see a true/false question that looks different, or off to you somehow, it is <u>probably false</u>. If you see an option on a multiple choice question that looks off or different, it is more than likely <u>not</u> the correct answer.
- **Always write neatly.**

<u>**Avoid Stress! Study, ask questions, and take a deep breath when you begin to feel anxious.**</u>

How to Study Smart for a Test
The Specifics

1. **Get organized with <u>what, when and where</u> to study.**

   ➢ You should not study everything your teacher gave to you in class; you should study what is most important….what your teachers have identified as important through notes, lectures, and study guides. <u>Study with a point, the main point.</u>

   ➢ The most effective way to retain information is to break up your studying over several days.

   ➢ Determine how many days you have to prepare, and then create a <u>plan</u> for what you are going to cover in each study session. For example, write in your assignment notebook that you are going to do a concept map for the information in chapter 2 on Monday, immediately after dinner. Tuesday, you will review the map and make note cards for vocabulary, etc...

   ➢ Know your schedule. If you are in the midst of a play, or have a big game on Wednesday, arrange your plan around those events. These activities can easily become distractions, but a little bit of planning will allow you to put your best effort into both studying and your activities.

   ➢ Determine the best place to study
   - Find a comfortable place to sit where all your materials can be easily displayed and within reach.
   - Make sure that you minimize distractions including phone, internet, and music.
   - If you feel the need to have some noise use something you will not be tempted to sing along with, tap your pencil to etc… Music can be a good mode of relaxation, but you need to pick music that will not create a distraction for you during the thinking and learning process.

2. **Know if you learn best through information presented visually, kinesthetically or auditorally.** (You can use the information provided earlier in this text to help you understand more about your learning style.)

   ➤ Visual learners should:

   Be more active in redesigning the materials in order to have a visual component. Color-coding, cluster mapping or grouping, drawing pictures, and making note cards are all excellent tools.

   ➤ Auditory learners should:

   Record pieces of information on a tape and listen to the information. It will help to couple the recordings and the written material, to help integrate them in your memory. Also it may be helpful for you to make up tests and quizzes for yourself. Doing something constructive as you read, such as annotating or drawing.

   ➤ Kinesthetic Learners should:

   Do something active with the material. Create charts and graphs. Walk around as you memorize materials. Make puzzles out of information to put together as a method of creating links between information.

3. **Participate in your learning. Know the difference between passive and active studying.**

   - Passive – reading over your notes
   - Active – doing something constructive as you read, such as annotating or drawing.

4. **Be proactive –**

   - Be an advocate for yourself. If you don't know what is going to be covered on a test ask questions in class with that in mind. Be direct and don't be afraid to speak up.
   - Set up meetings with teachers, tutors, or mentors to help you get prepared.

5. **Do not cram!**
    - Cramming is the worst yet most commonly used study habit. Your short term memory is the only portion of you brain used when cramming, and research shows that part of memory can hold only approximately 7-10 bits of information at a <u>single time</u>.
    - Working with the material actively, and in small increments over several days, will feel less like studying, but be a more effective way to retain the information!

6. <u>**Study for the type of test you are having**</u>:

   ➢ Multiple choice and true/false, objective assessments:

   Study   Definitions and terms
   Lists of items
   Make up some false statements

   ➢ Essay Tests:
   Stress more large concepts
   Study   List and answer probable questions
   When practicing answers, prepare a cluster map or an outline

   ➢ Problem Exams
   Study   Memorize formulas
   Practice Problems

How do I remember all this information?
Understanding Memory

General overview of how memory works:

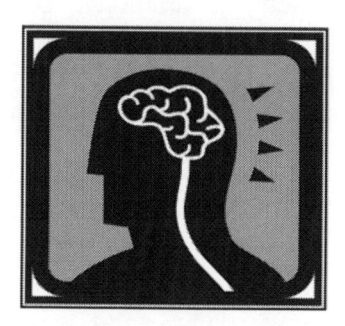

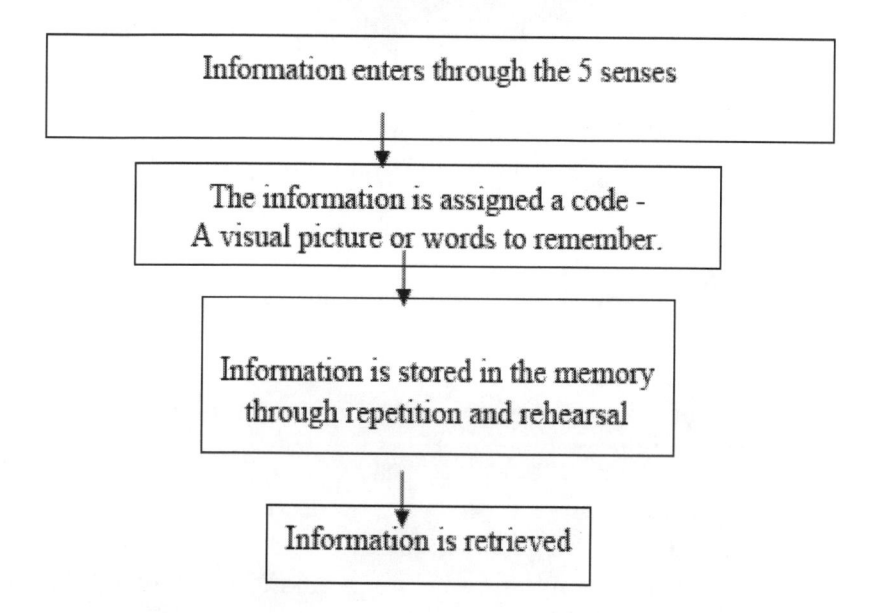

```
Information enters through the 5 senses
                   ↓
The information is assigned a code -
A visual picture or words to remember.
                   ↓
Information is stored in the memory
through repetition and rehearsal
                   ↓
Information is retrieved
```

Memory is a tricky thing. One minute it is your friend the next your foe. To help yourself develop a good working memory you need to develop good retrieval cues. To do so you should review often, say the information out loud, and practice, practice, practice.

How do we get the information to stick where we want it?

➢ *Mnemonics & Acronyms*- Create silly words or rhymes to remember pertinent information. The old standby example is ROY G. BIV to remember the colors of the rainbow. Use the first letter of every concept you need to remember and then create a silly sentence with those letters.

➢ *"Chunking"*- When trying to remember groups of information chunk it together and make a label. For example, if you need to learn all the food groups in French, chunk (or group) the information together to demonstrate each section of the food group. Put all the dairy products in one group with a picture of a milk jug at the top, and all the fruits in another, etc...

➢ We remember things best when the information <u>means something to us</u>. Try to learn the concepts in <u>your terms</u>. Relate the material to an experience or write/talk out your understanding of the concept in your own words.

➢ *Remembering vocabulary*- Vocabulary is very specific. The best way to remember a definition is to write it, rewrite, make flash cards, color code similar concepts, and repeat them out loud. Repetition is the key to retaining vocabulary and basic facts.

➢ *Comprehension*- It is always easier to remember something we understand. Make sure the concepts make sense to you. Rephrase them in language you would use, combined with pertinent vocabulary.

➢ *Test Yourself. Study in groups where you are ACTIVELY sharing information, testing each other, playing games…..*

The Big Day

- Get enough sleep so that you are well rested.
- Make sure that you eat prior to going to school.
- Enter the test with confidence.
- When the teacher hands out the test flip it over and write down any acronyms, mnemonics, formulas, dates, facts or ideas you are afraid you might forget.
- Read the directions twice before beginning the test.

Helpful hints for specific types of tests:

Problem Solving	Essay	True/False	Multiple Choice	Short Answer	Matching
Make sure you check all signs	Read and reread the question.	Read the entire statement.	Try to answer the question without looking at the choices first	Get clues from the words used in the question.	Cross out words after you use them.
Rewrite the signs and labels in a different color when checking it over	Underline key components. Number each part of the question you need to address.	Questions with _always_ and _never_ are usually false.	Read all your choices before selecting the correct one.	Answers are usually specific in nature.	Make sure each answer can only be used once.
	Be aware of time limits and put yourself on a time schedule	Fact or opinion? Facts are true opinions are false.	Underline key parts of the question.	If you are not 100% sure, pack as much pertinent information as possible into the answer	Reread the statement in combination with your answer to make sure it makes sense.
	Develop and outline before you begin to write.	Every part of the statement needs to be true.	Cross out each answer you know is not the correct one.		
	Pack in as much information as you can.	If in doubt – guess "true".			
	Worry about content more than sentence structure…	If the sentence doesn't look or read right it is most likely false.			

Test Anxiety

Fact or Fiction?

Test anxiety is a normal phenomenon in that most people feel some level of elevated stress and anxiety over evaluations and/or exams. This often indicates our desire to do well at something we care about or are invested in. So, when does anxiety cross over from a normal occurrence to a concern? When it begins to adversely affect your ability to perform. The term test anxiety can really be best described as a performance anxiety. The term anxiety creates issues for some people in education, parents, and in many children – so it may be more appropriate to describe it as a difficulty demonstrating what a student has learned. For sake of clarity we will use test anxiety in further discussions.

How do you know if you have test anxiety and what are some of the signs?

- Difficulty concentrating
- Difficulty sleeping prior to exams
- Perspiration, or sweaty palms
- Rapid, shallow breathing
- Rapid heart beats, increased blood pressure
- Nausea, upset stomach, digestion slows down
- Headache, muscle tension
- Typical reactions of those with test anxiety:
    - "I felt I was ready for the test, but my mind just went blank."
    - "Before the test I started to feel sick. I just wanted to get out of there."

- "I thought I did fine but when I got my test back I got a 'D', I don't know what happened?"
- "I kept thinking what was going to happen if I failed this test? I just know I am going to fail this test."
- "If I keep failing tests I will never get into a good college."

The physical symptoms of anxiety are created by the sympathetic nervous system. That is the portion of the nervous system that gets us excited. In the process, it also releases adrenaline which excites the muscles and gets us going. While heading into a testing situation you want some of this to occur, as it will help you to feel confident. Avoiding test anxiety is a fine balance between the sympathetic and parasympathetic nervous systems. The parasympathetic system helps to calm us down. The key to monitoring test nervousness and keeping it from becoming test anxiety is mastering this balance.

Adverse effects of test anxiety:

> **Nervousness can cause some of the following to occur:**

- Lower rate of reading comprehension
- Sequential and organization thinking may decrease
- Word retrieval may fail or slow
- Focus and concentration may become hampered

> **Mental Blocking:**

- Going "blank" on questions
- Ability to recall all the information once the testing situation is over

What causes test anxiety?

- **Test Preparation skills:**
  - Poor study strategies
  - Cramming
  - Poor time management
  - Disorganization of materials and test subject matter
  - Not asking questions in class (or out of class) when confused about a topic.

- **Test anxiety is also compounded by worrying:**
  - Attitudes and beliefs determine how we act. (self-talk is critical)
  - Thinking about past performance on tests
  - How other students are performing on the test, and how quickly they complete the test.
  - Negative consequences of failure
  - Social and family pressures
  - Test anxiety is a <u>learned response</u> (you must look at the environment for clues in reducing anxiety)

So, if you know what it is, what it looks like, and how it can sometimes be created, how do you cope with it?

- **Identify what anxiety looks like for you:**
  - What triggers your anxiety?
  - What physical symptoms do you have?
  - What type of conversations are you having with yourself?
  - What are the environmental expectations placed upon you?

➤ **Identify study strategies that are effective for you:**
- Study in short stints for several nights before exam.
- Mapping, outlining, color-coding, note-cards, etc.
- Use your time effectively – do not procrastinate. It will lead to cramming which will exacerbate your anxiety level.

➤ **Master your anxiety:**
- Do not allow your anxiety to create a snowball effect – **interrupt it!**
- Find relaxation techniques that work for you – and remember nothing usually works immediately, so don't give up.
- Practice positive talk strategies to combat negative self-statement.
- Remember, after all, it is just a test.
- Use your tense feelings to alert you to oncoming anxiety.
- When fear takes control and you panic – interrupt the flow.
- Focus on the present, the here and now, not the future.

Reducing your anxiety is a two step process. First, take steps to prevent the anxiety from occurring. Second, realize that prevention is not full proof, and have a plan of action to combat anxiety.

➤ **Prevention:**
- Organize your time and materials before studying.
- Break study sessions up into several shorter period verses long cramming sessions.
- Practice visualization and relaxation techniques.

- **Develop some coping strategies:**
  - Physical Relaxation-
    For 30-60 seconds at a time try to totally relax your muscles physically. It may help to tighten all your muscles for 10-20 seconds, release them, exhale, and then completely relax for 30-60 seconds.

  - Use positive self-talk strategies-
    Avoid negative self-talk. Prepare key words or phrases that you can repeat to yourself to refocus and calm yourself down. Negative statements will only heighten your anxiety level.

- **Manage the test-**
  - Plan on using the entire time allotted for the test session.

  - Stop, pause, and relax when you begin to feel anxiety creeping in.

  - After you have answered all the questions you know immediately go back and try to figure the others out. If you are having difficulty recalling information for one of the questions, it is okay to skip it again and go back. Continually trying to recall a frustrating question will only elevate your feelings of anxiousness.

  - Do Something! If you cannot think of a proper response don't just sit there. Draw the concept to help you get organized, use cognitive mapping techniques, say some positive statements to yourself, or do some relaxation techniques.

Additional techniques that will help you feel more prepared for tests:

- **Engage in <u>active reading</u>:**
  - Pre-read or scan information

- Use study techniques such as outlining, annotating, mapping, flashcards, etc.
- Write your own test questions as you read – what would you ask if you were the teacher.
- Read out load
- Draw a picture to help you retain the concept of information.
- Discuss the material with peers; participate in a study group.
- When reading test questions identify key words and phrases. (Example: directive words - identify, describe, etc…)

➢ **Memory Techniques:**
- Spread study time out over several short sessions, because it helps to transfer the information into your long-term memory.
- Cramming – don't do it! Cramming puts information into your short-term memory. Your short term memory can only hold approximately 7-10 pieces of information for minimal time limits & when information is held in your long term memory it is easier to recall.
- Make the goal to over-learn the material.
- Teach the concepts to others.
- Develop your own examples that make sense to you.
- Write practice essays.

➢ <u>**Do not participate in irrational thinking**</u>!
- Identify your irrational belief system.
- Examine and dispute your irrational beliefs.
- Allow yourself to take charge.

- Create your own set of goals.
- Remember whatever you get on a test is not the worst thing that can happen to you in life.

V.

Other pearls

A Few Other Pearls

What do you do if you miss a day of class?

1. If you know you are going to miss school ahead of time let each teacher know you will not be in class. (If you don't want to discuss the reason in detail, simply say, for personal reasons, medical reasons, something general but be <u>truthful</u>.)
   - Ask what information will be covered in class.
   - Ask for any pertinent handouts
   - Ask about homework assignments.
   - Determine a timeframe for when any missed assignment or test will be completed and returned to the teacher.
2. If you miss due to illness or emergency:
   - Immediately upon returning to school, set up a time to meet with each teacher.
   - Identify what was missed and if there were any handouts, etc…
   - Set a time for when the missed work will be expected to be turned in or by when any tests should be completed.

***If you are out for an extended period of time make sure that your counselor is aware so they can help you to manage the academic strain that may occur. If your teachers have email, it may be helpful to communicate with them on a regular basis while you are out.

> ### Things not to do:
>
> 1. Use your absence as an excuse to fall further behind.
> 2. Expect your teacher to seek you out.
> 3. Just blow off the assignment.
> 4. Let yourself get overwhelmed and not ask for help.

What to do if you are having trouble in class?

1. <u>Talk</u> to your teacher.
2. <u>Talk</u> to your parents.
3. <u>Talk</u> to your counselor.
4. <u>Talk</u> to your classmates.

Getting the point yet? TALK **TALK TALK until someone can help you.

Procrastinators – this is for you.

1. Determine if your procrastination is a habit that runs throughout your life or is it situation specific? For example, do you procrastinate only when you have to write an English paper?
2. On projects of any kind **<u>Develop a Plan</u>**
    - Break the assignment/task into manageable steps.
    - Create a timeline for when you plan to get each piece done.
    - Build in a way to reward yourself for staying on schedule and a consequence for not sticking to your timeline.
    - Have a plan for if you fall behind your schedule.

3. Identify emotions that you have around the issue of procrastination.
4. Determine the things that are within your control to change.
5. Visualize yourself as successful.

<u>Take each project one at a time. The more often you create a plan of action, the more successes you will have. This pattern of success will help you to procrastinate less.</u>

"I can't concentrate?"

Concentration is often believed to be one of those things that is out of our control. For a majority of people, and situations, this is false. We must teach ourselves how to concentrate in school, when studying, when participating in sports, music, art, etc... There are some basic things that we can all do to help us pay attention.

- When studying, create an environment for yourself free of distractions.
- Have a consistent routine for all tasks that require concentration.
- When you catch yourself drifting have a verbal cue for yourself to snap you back on task.
- Active learning can help you to focus better, and stay involved. **Get Active.**
- Remind yourself to focus.

Setting goals can help you achieve:

Setting goals allow you plan your pathway to success. Goals are individually driven and something you can develop for school, extra curricular activities, and your future.

<u>Short Term Goals</u>: can be anything within the immediate timeframe, such as a test at the end of the week, a specific assignment, etc...

<u>Long Term Goals</u>: should encompass smaller goals which reach out over a longer distance in time such as overall GPA, semester grade, etc…

Once you have determined some goals make sure they meet these three standards:

- Measurable
- Specific
- Obtainable

    Ex. I will surpass my B average in Italian and get an A for the semester.

Next: **create a plan of action.**

I will meet this goal of getting an A in Italian by doing the following things:

- I will make note cards for vocabulary on a weekly basis.
- I will write down confusing concepts and meet with a study group or my teacher to review them.
- I will set up periodic sessions with my teacher to review my progress.

Get involved!

There is no doubt that students involved within the school setting are more likely to feel success and connection within the school environment. School activities create a safe haven for students and foster skills of leadership, independence and skill building. Activities will not only help you to enjoy your high school experience, but also to make connections to various students and staff members you may not have otherwise met.

Understand the Basics of High School:

Transcript: This is the document that records your grades, classes you have taken, test scores reported to the school, GPA/Class rank, and your anticipated graduation date. While these are typical, you may see some variation from school to school. Simply put, this is a record of your high school academic experience.

Class Rank: This shows where you rank against other students in your graduating class.

GPA: Your grade point average, or GPA, is the process by which your letter grades are given a numerical value and then averaged. This can be done on a semester, yearly, and/or overall basis. The higher your grades are the higher your average is. Below is a common example of how this is computed on a 4 point scale:

$$A=4$$
$$B=3$$
$$C=2$$
$$D=1$$

*A student who earns 50% B's 50% C's would have a 2.5 GPA

Example:

Algebra	- B (3)
English	- C (2)
Chemistry	- B (3)
World History	- C (2)

3+2+3+2 = 10 / 4 classes = 2.5 GPA

Honors/AP type classes are often weighted differently; making 5 points the highest you can attain in such a class.

Transcripts reflect your academic successes and failures. Upward trends, or steady grades, reflect more positively to post graduate options than a downward trend. Just a little something to keep in mind. Grades really do matter all the way through your high school experience.

A note about high school social life and the roller coaster ride.

Let's face it, being a teenager can be filled with drama. Friends and relationships may come and go. Big dances may come and go without a date. You might not make the team, the play, the band, or be accepted in the club. You get the point? You will fail a test; you may even fall down or drop your tray in the cafeteria. Some say being a teenager is the best time in your life! There will be days you will think whoever said that was insane, or so old they don't remember what it was like. Social situations may put you in many difficult positions requiring you to make uncomfortable decisions. You will make good choices in school and outside of it. More than likely you will also make poor ones you may regret. Just remember this – <u>don't be afraid to talk to trusted adults</u> available to help you deal with some of the life struggles you will face. Remember that even with all the pitfalls, <u>life will go on</u> and your grades will play a major part in the direction it can take.

Concerns about peer or self safety:

Today as teenagers you have seen and heard of many scary situations from around the country and the world. If you feel you are in an unsafe situation, school related or not, do not remain quiet. There are many professionals in your building to support you, in many different ways. Use them, use your family if you can, but remember that <u>a silent voice cannot make changes</u>. If you have concerns about a friend or peer, for their personal safety or that of others, remember the most important thing you can do is talk to an adult. Do not try to deal with difficult situations by yourself. Some adolescents deal with a lot of issues, including depression, isolation, anger, eating disorders and problems with drugs and alcohol to name a few. Not everyone will encounter someone in these situations, and thankfully not everyone will have to deal with these situations in their own life. However, everyone can be aware they exist and be a voice for someone else who may be in need of help.

A Note about Teachers:

- Most teachers are in this field because they love their subject, they love to work with kids, they love to educate.

- Be respectful of their time and effort.

- Remember you are not their only student – schedule an appointment.

- If you want to speak with them after class ask them politely if they have a minute.

- Remember they have lives outside of school as well – they are not at your beckoned call.

Included in the following pages are the specifics you will want to know about your school and your individual experience there. There are questions you will need to ask your counselor to ensure you begin your journey through High School on the right path.

Your High School Information

Counselor's Name: _____
Principal's Name: _____

Pertinent email addresses:

Freshman Year	**Sophomore Year**	**Junior Year**	**Senior Year**

Your School Specifics

The attendance policy is:

The tardy policy is:

Eligibility for extra curricular participation requirements are:

Dress codes:

Other pertinent rules:

Graduation requirements:

Number of credits/courses required overall:

Number of credits in each area:	Required	Recommended
English	_____	_____
Math	_____	_____
Science	_____	_____
Social Sciences	_____	_____
Fine and Applied Arts	_____	_____
Foreign Language	_____	_____

Your School Schedule

Freshman	Sophomore	Junior	Senior
Semester 1	Semester 1	Semester 1	Semester 1
Semester 2	Semester 2	Semester 2	Semester 2

Notes

Everyone will fall down, fail a test, forget an assignment – those who will be successful accept this and <u>learn from it</u>!

K. Donay

References

Some material presented in this guide was adapted from the following resources:

Andrea M. Lazzari & Judy W. Wood. <u>125 Ways to be a better test-taker</u>. E. Moline, Illinois. Linquisystems. 1994

Jeanne Shay Schumm and Marguertie Radencich, <u>School Power</u>. Minneapolis Minnesota. Free Spirit Publishing. 1992

Marty Super. <u>Crash Course for Study Skills</u>. E. Moline, Illinois. Linquisystems. 1993

<u>"Stress and Anxiety resources"</u> developed by the University of Buffalo, Counseling center.

About the Author

Kristi Reirden Donay, Ed.S, is a certified school psychologist. She obtained her Bachelors degree from the University of Evansville, with a focus on secondary education in the fields of sociology, psychology, and history. The combination of Division I volleyball and a demanding academic schedule taught her strong skills in the areas of organization, planning, time management and goal setting. Using these skills she continued her education, obtaining a Masters degree and an Educational Specialist degree in the field of school psychology from Kent State University. Kristi has spent the past fourteen years working with children and adolescents in the gym or the classroom, as an educator, a traditional school psychologist, an intervention specialist, and a volleyball coach. For the last six years she concentrated on her work with adolescents in the public school system. Supporting teachers, families, and students throughout the education process has always been her focus. This is her first book. Kristi is married with two young sons, and is currently continuing to write and do research in the field of education and family dynamics.

Made in the USA
Lexington, KY
10 June 2014